I HATE to READ!
A Stomp and Play Book

by Stacy Hoffer

Illustration by Genevieve LaVO Cosdon

With gratitude to my husband and sons for their incredible support,
I dedicate this book to every human being who has a brain that is
wired differently. Never give up, or discount your unique gifts and talents.
You are here to change the world for the better. Rock on! — Stacy Hoffer

For my little loves, Dashiell and Margaux — Genevieve LaVO Cosdon

Balboa Press books may be ordered through booksellers or by contacting:

Balboa Press
A Division of Hay House
1663 Liberty Drive
Bloomington, IN 47403
www.balboapress.com
1 (877) 407-4847

Because of the dynamic nature of the Internet, any web addresses or links contained in this book may have changed since publication and may no longer be valid. The views expressed in this work are solely those of the author and do not necessarily reflect the views of the publisher, and the publisher hereby disclaims any responsibility for them.

Cover and book design by Genevieve LaVO Cosdon
The text for this book is set in Dyslexie.
The illustrations for this book are rendered in oil pastel.

ISBN: 978-1-9822-0055-8 (sc)
ISBN: 978-1-9822-0056-5 (e)

Library of Congress Control Number: 2018905786

Print information available on the last page.

Balboa Press rev. date: 06/05/2018

BALBOA.
PRESS
A DIVISION OF HAY HOUSE

A Note to Parents

My dear fellow parents,

I am guessing that you probably don't much like the title of this book. Perhaps you detest it, or find it offensive, although I am sure you don't HATE it. ;)

As a psychotherapist for the past 25 years, I have noticed that many parents do not want their kids to use the word "hate", saying it is "too strong" and "could hurt someone's feelings".

I agree that "hate" is a strong word, like "love", but of course we don't discourage our kids from using the word "love". Why is that? Perhaps if we say we hate something it feels like the worst possible thing to say, and it implies a static state of being. "I hate broccoli!" or "I hate my sixth grade teacher!", or "I hate to read!" But as we all know, feelings are anything but static. Even if a child hates something or someone this morning, it could change by dinner time. "Hate" is just a word that vividly expresses a child's anger, rage, frustration and helplessness.

Think about it this way: What seven year old will come home to her mother, sit down calmly, and say, "Mother, I must tell you that reading is very stressful and exhausting for me. Sometimes words move on the page. I can't stay focused. I am so busy trying to decode the words that I lose the bigger meaning of the story. It seems like everyone in my class can do it much quicker and easier than me, which makes me feel quite inadequate and unintelligent. Reading aloud makes me feel humiliated and out of control." What do we get instead? We see our child throw his books on the floor, delay doing his homework in every way possible (like volunteering to clean the toilet instead), throwing fits, getting a headache, and/or collapsing in tears.

So the child that shrieks, "I hate to read!" is expressing his feelings in an age appropriate manner. I implore you not to shut this down, because the child is "using her words" as many of us parents have diligently coached our children to do. In this book, I have gone a step beyond words. I invite parents and kids to use the STOMP sign to stop and sing, which is a way to physically express intense feelings that is safe, humorous, and completely acceptable. You will find that the STOMP & sing is a resource you and your child can use in many different situations, and it will give your child a real sense of empowerment when facing any academic challenge.

Yours in Imperfection,
Stacy Hoffer, LCSW

Harriet Anastasia "Stacy" Hoffer, MA, M.Div, MSW, LCSW
Princeton, NJ 08540
609-865-9902
Stacy.Hoffer0703@gmail.com

I hate to read; I don't know why, but it is very true. And since you're looking at this book, it might be true for you. I'm glad I'm not the only one who hates these words so much.

These letters are like naughty dogs or pots too hot to touch!

So welcome to my little book! I hope you'll come along, and whenever it gets to be too much, stop and sing the song.

Try it now, and you will see it's really fun to do:

Just stomp your feet and shout the words.
It feels so good to move!

Boring, Boring, Boring,
Reading is SO Boring!
Boring, Boring, Boring,
I really hate to read!

There you go! Try it again.
Maybe a third time too?

Don't worry how you look or sound,
they won't put you in the zoo!
Now that you're ready, let's go on.
Bid this page adieu, and I will
show you all the things
I would rather do...

Ask awful ogres
for directions,

or prep rowdy red beets
for inspection.

Bite a rotten, blistered berry,

or tickle werewolves 'til they're merry.

Creep up on criminal candy canes,

or make mad hatters go insane.

Dive in a pool of roasted onions,

or let angry alligators chew my bunions.

Exercise with stinky skunks,

or help my **N**ana to go punk.

Fly to Finland on a lamp,

or fix a feast of postage stamps.

Grant three wishes to a grape,

or give a bath to grumpy snakes.

Hop around in bitter broth,

or swim upstream with three-toed sloths.

Invite a kangaroo to tea,

or imitate a chimpanzee.

Judge a jellyfishing race,

or joust a king from outer space.

Knit a top hat for a fly,

or sing rotten rats a lullaby.

THIS IS AWFUL!

Boring, Boring, Boring,
Reading is SO Boring!
Boring, Boring, Boring,
I really hate to read!

I would rather...

Lasso up a lightning bolt,

or let my pet rocks ride a colt.

Melt a mound of moldy cheese,

or munch on marble apple trees.

Nab some naughty nightingales,

or catch a bunch of slimy snails.

Open vats of smelly oil,

or plant candy seeds in magic soil.

Pester zombies to come play,

or pounce on porcupines all day!

It would be much more fun to...

or let frogs frolic in my pants.

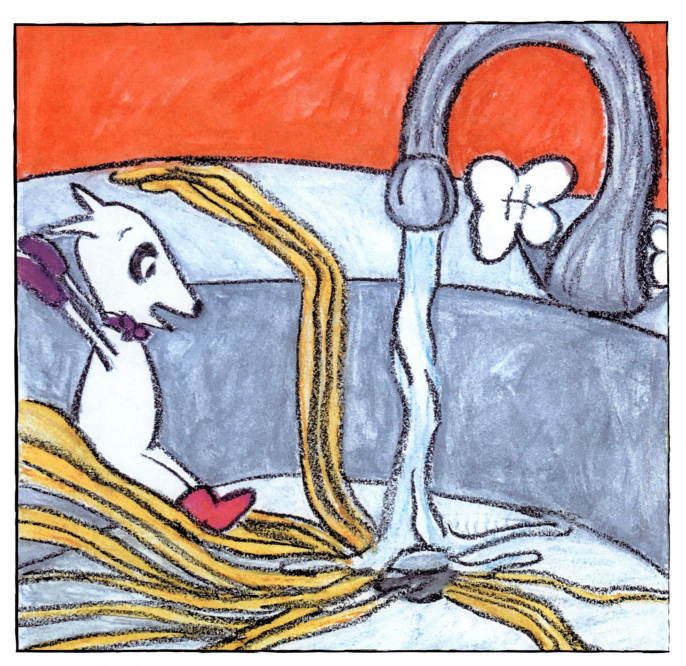

Ride pasta ribbons down the drain,

or listen to prickly pears complain.

Sneak a bite
of cauliflower,

or suck some candy that's too sour.

Tickle lots of hairy creatures,

or twist my face
into freaky features.

Unleash a stalk of killer kale,

or take merry monkeys out to sail.

Vault in a field of putrid peas,

Wipe a whining wombat's nose,

or pick up thumb tacks with your toes?

X-ray old gray grumpy cats,

Yell at jumping jelly beans,

or hassle hyenas until they scream?

Zip around in chocolate cars,

or zap aliens with lemon bars?

Now our funny book is done! I hope you know it's true, that I absolutely hate to read, I really, really do. So the next time words are getting you down, and reading feels all wrong, you can get up and move around, and STOMP,

and sing the song! Would you like to try it one more time?

Printed in the United States
By Bookmasters